Standard Spanish (Colombian) Manual.

180 Expressions you must know!

Andrea Castellanos

Standard Spanish (Colombian) Manual. 180 Expressions you must know!

Standard Spanish (Colombian) Manual. 180 Expressions you must know!

Being monolingual seems to be disadvantageous in our multicultural society. Our current world is more culturally demanding every day. The most popular statement has become "I wish I knew how to say...in Spanish/French/German"

This book will focus on helping you communicate in Spanish without your google translator and to develop and increase everyday expressions you can easily use with other human beings. This book is meant to be for people who want to communicate with Spanish speakers in different work/social situations.

Dedication Page

To all the human beings who wished they could install different language applications in their minds, to just open them whenever is necessary.

Also, to some colleagues and other professionals who took some time to answer the question I texted them, "Could you please send me some work/social expressions you wished you knew in Spanish?"

TABLE OF CONTENTS

Chapter 1: Expressions Teachers may Use with Students........8

Chapter 2: Expressions Teachers May Use with Parents.........11

Chapter 3: Working as a waiter/ in the kitchen...................15

Chapter 4: Expressions for any other social......................18

Chapter 5: Idioms (Idiomatic Expressions).......................24

Chapter 6: Business Expressions..................................27

Chapter 7: Travel...31

Chapter 8: At the restaurant (Food)..............................34

Chapter 1

Chapter 1: Expressions Teachers may Use with Students (Classroom commands)

Capítulo 1:Expresiones que los profesores o maestros pueden usar con sus estudiantes

1. Sit down.	Siéntate por favor.
2. Be quiet.	Callado (Talking to a male).

3. Be quiet.	Callada (Talking to a female).
4. Listen.	Escucha.
5.Be respectful.	Se respetuoso.
6.Work on your assignment.	Haz tu trabajo.
7. Do you have a pencil or do you need one?	¿Tienes lápiz o necesitas uno?
8. How may I help you?	¿Cómo puedo ayudarte?
9. Do you understand what you have to do/must do/should do?	¿Entiendes lo que tienes que hacer?
10.Explicame lo que debes hacer?	Explain to me what you have to do/ must do/should do?

11. What should/must you do? What do you have to do?	¿Qué deberías estar haciendo?
12. What 's your name?	¿Cómo te llamas? ¿Cuál es tu nombre?
13. My name is/ I am…	Mi nombre es/soy…
14. How are you today? What's up?	¿Cómo estás hoy? ¿Cómo te sientes hoy?
15. I am proud of you (male saying it).	Estoy orgulloso de ti.
16. I am proud of you (female saying it).	Estoy orgullosa de ti.
17. Sharpen your pencil	Sácale punta a tu lápiz
18. Where is your stuff?	¿Dónde están tus cosas?
19. Who are you hanging out with?	¿Con quién te la pasas?
20. Who are you talking to?	¿A quién le hablas? ¿A quién le estás hablando?

Chapter 2

Chapter 2: Expressions Teachers May Use with Parents

Capítulo 2:Expresiones que los profesores pueden usar con padres

1.How are you? I am… (student's name teacher)	¿Cómo está? Yo soy la maestra/ profesora de… (Student 's name)
2. I want to talk to you because…	Quiero hablar con usted porque…

3. What is your phone number?	¿Cuál es su número de teléfono?
4.How is your son/daughter doing?	¿Cómo ha estado su hijo/hija? ¿Cómo ha estado ____? (student 's name).
5.How are you guys doing?	¿Cómo han estado ustedes? ¿Cómo están ustedes?
6. (Student's name) ____is pretty smart, he/ she just needs to work on…	(Start with a student 's name) Padro es muy inteligente, solo necesita mejorar en…
7. We, teachers, are going to use CLASSDOJO to reach out to parents. That is why we need your phone number.	Vamos a utilizar CLASSDOJO para comunicarnos con los padres por eso necesitamos su número de teléfono, por favor.
8.Do you have any questions?	¿Tiene alguna pregunta?
9.How can/may I help you?	¿Cómo puedo ayudarle?

10. Whatever you need, just let me know.	Cualquier cosa que necesite por favor déjeme saber.
11.Let's keep in touch.	Estamos hablando.
12. It is a pleasure to have your son/daughter in this class.	Es un gusto tener a su hijo/hija (male/female) en esta clase.
13. I need your help, so your son/daughter can learn.	Necesito su ayuda para que su hijo/hija pueda aprender.
14. It is my pleasure/You're welcome.	Con mucho gusto/ de nada.
15. This is what she/he has to do in Math/Reading.	Esto es lo que tiene que hacer en Matemáticas/Lectura.
16. Let me explain.	Déjeme explicarle.
17.The idea would be…	La idea sería…

18. The homework is…	La tarea es…
19. The other (female) teacher is…	La otra maestra/profesora es…
20. The other (male) teacher is…	El otro maestro/profesor es…

Notes

Chapter 3

Chapter 3: Working as a waiter/waitress in the kitchen

Capítulo 3:Trabajando de mesero/mesera en la cocina

1.Where are the pans/dishes/plates/spoons/bowls/ladles?	¿ Dónde están las ollas/platos/cucharas/cucharones?
2. What orders are pending?	¿ Qué ordenes tenemos pendientes?
3. How may I help?	¿ Qué más puedo hacer para ayudar?
4.What would you like to order?	¿ Qué le gustaría pedir/ordenar?

5. I would recommend (food/drink).	Yo le recomendaría…
6. My favorite food is… because…	Mi plato favorito es… porque
7.Could you pass me a spoon/pan/napkin on, please?	Pasame una cuchara/olla/servilleta, por favor.
8. Hand a fork,plate,ladle to me please.	Pásame un tenedor/plato/cucharón, por favor.
9. Give me the sugar or rice container, please.	Pásame el azúcar/el arroz, por favor.
10. Hand the salt/pepper/lettuce to me.	Pásame la sal/pimienta/la lechuga.
11. Pass me the potatoes, please.	Pásame las papas, por favor.
12. Help me clean/do the dishes/cook/pass something/serve/take care of clients/fry/warm up, please.	Ayúdame a limpiar/lavar los platos/cocinar/pasar/servir/atender/freír/ fritar/calentar, por favor.
13. This is your food.	Traje su comida

14. What would you like to drink?	¿ Qué le gustaría beber/tomar?
15. We have water, orange juice/ Strawberry/pineapple/melon/ grape juice.	Tenemos agua, jugo de naranja/fresa/piña/melón/uva.
16. We also have lemonade/beer/cocktails like…	También tenemos limonada/cerveza/ cocteles como…
17. Thanks for coming, we hope to have you back soon.	Gracias por venir, esperamos que vuelva.
18. How was the food?	¿ Cómo le pareció la comida?
19. How was the food?	Puedes hacer la ensalada/ fritar/ freir las papas/la carne
20. What do you know how to cook?	¿ Qué sabes cocinar?

Chapter 4

Chapter 4: Expressions for any other social situations

Capítulo 4:Expresiones para cualquier otra situación social.

People from South America may use "usted o tu" (You) interchangeably. Colombians may prefer "tu" formal/informal because it shows more familiarity.

1. I have no idea.	No tengo ni idea.
2. What's your name? My name is/ I am…	¿Cómo te llamas?¿Cuál es tu nombre? Mi nombre es/soy
3. Do you have any plans for today/tomorrow/the summer/the spring/the fall/the weekend/Monday/within fifteen days?	¿Tienes planes para hoy/mañana/ el verano/la primavera/ el otoño/ el fin de semana/ el lunes/en quince días?
4.Let 's have a drink today. Do you want to have a drink today?	Vamos a tomarnos algo hoy. ¿Vamos a tomarnos algo hoy?
5. What is your phone number?	¿Cuál es tu número de teléfono?
6.How is it going? How are you? (Talking to a stranger or someone you just became acquainted with)	¿Cómo está todo?, ¿Cómo va la vida? ¿Cómo le va?

7. How is it going? (Talking to a close friend or relative).	¿Cómo estás? ¿Cómo vas? ¿Cómo te ha ido?
8. You look pretty well.	Te ves muy bien.
9. You look pretty good in that outfit.	Te ves muy bonita vestida así.
10. It is so nice to see you.	Me da gusto verte.
11. That looks tasty/yummy.	Se ve delicioso.
12. I like your outfit.	Me encanta tu vestimenta.
13. How is your family doing?	¿Cómo está tu familia?
14. Things like that.	Cosas como esas.
15. Long time no see.	Hace harto que no nos veíamos.
16. Sweet/great.	Que chevere.
17. What are you doing?	¿Qué estás haciendo?

18. What are you going to order? What are you ordering?	¿Qué vas a pedir?
19. What do you prefer?	¿Qué prefieres?
20. What time are you leaving?	¿A qué hora sales? ¿A qué hora te vas?
21. I want to invite her out.	Quiero invitarla a salir.
22. I would like to invite him on a date.	Me gustaría invitarlo a salir.
23. Someone broke in.	Se entraron a mi casa.
24. I want to invite you to my house/apartment. I want to invite you over.	Quiero invitarte a mi casa.
25. Come over, so we can work together.	Ven a mi casa y trabajamos juntos/ juntas (including a male and a female or just males/ including just females).

26. I will pick you up. Do you want me to pick you up?	Yo te recojo. Te recojo. ¿te recojo?
27.I will drop you off.	Yo te dejo allá.
28. What kind of food do you like? I like…	¿Qué clase de comida te gusta? Me gusta…
29. I get along well with you.	Me caes bien.
30. We don't get along.	No nos llevamos bien
31.You are gorgeous.	Eres bien bonita (Talking to a female).
32.You are handsome/hot.	Eres atractivo.
33.Head over to my condo.	Ven a mi apartamento.
34. I am excited to see you.	Estoy emocionado de verte (Male talking).
35.I am excited to see you.	Estoy emocionada de verte (Female talking).

36.I ran into her last time at the grocery store.	Me la encontré el otro día en el supermercado.
37.I ran into him yesterday.	Me lo encontré ayer.
38.They split up. They broke up. They got divorced.	Ellos se separaron.
39.She leads on. She pretends to agree with him/her He leads on.	Ella le lleva la idea. Él le lleva la idea.
40.She is a gold digger.	Es una interesada.

Chapter 5

Capítulo 5: Expresiones idiomáticas

1.I am swamped with work.	Estoy lleno (male) de trabajo.
	Llena (female) de trabajo.

2.The cats out of the bag/ Let the cats out of the bag/ Spill the beans.	Cuenta el chisme.
3. I thought you already knew. Don't spill the beans.	Pensé que ya sabías, no le cuentes a nadie.
4.It costs an arm and a leg.	Cuesta un ojo de la cara.
5.Better late than never.	Más vale tarde que nunca.
6. Break a leg.	Buena suerte.
7. Don't allow it to get out of hand.	No dejes que eso se te salga de las manos.
8. Calm down.	Relajate.
9.Speak of the devil.	Hablando del rey de Roma.
10.Time flies when you're having fun.	El tiempo vuela.
11. I feel under the weather today.	Estoy enfermo (male). Estoy enferma (female).

12. A bird in the hand is worth two in the bush.	Más vale pájaro en mano que ciento volando.
13. Don't cry over spilt milk.	No llores sobre la leche derramada.
14. Don't put all your eggs in one basket.	No hay que poner todos los huevos en una canasta.
15. He's a chip off the old block.	Igualito a ti (talking about a male). Igualita a ti (Talking about a female).
16.Kill to birds with one stone.	Mata dos pájaros de un solo tiro.
17. Once in a blue moon.	Rara vez.
18.The early bird gets the worm.	Al que madruga Dios le ayuda.
19.This matter is a storm in a teacup.	Estás haciendo una tormenta en un vaso de agua.
20.Come rain or shine.	Llueva, truene o relampaguee.

Chapter 6

Capítulo 6: Expresiones de negocios

Realtors Vendedores de finca raíz.

1. How long have you been searching for homes?	Por cuánto tiempo ha estado buscando una casa?

2. What kind of house are you looking for? How many rooms? how many bathrooms	Quétipo de casa está buscando?Cuántas habitaciones? Cuántos baños
3. When do you want to buy?	En cuánto tiempo espera comprar?
4.Have you found financing yet?	Ya encontró alguien que la financie?
5. Do you need a lender?	Necesita financiación?
6.Give me the big picture.	Cuéntamelo todo.
7. Let's get down to business.	Pongámonos serios y hagamos lo que tenemos que hacer
8. Let 's go the extra mile.	Hagamos más de lo esperado.

9. My hands are tied.	Nada que yo pueda hacer.
10. No-brainer.	Nada fuera de lo común.
11. You are putting the cart before the horse.	Está ensillando la burra sin tener yeguas paridas.
12. We are all in the same boat.	Todos estamos en el mismo bote. Estamos todos en las mismas.
13. I took the bull by the horns.	Tomé el toro por los cachos.
14. That is an uphill battle.	Eso está de para arriba.
15. Are we on the same page?	Estamos de acuerdo?
16. They talked me into it.	Ellos me convencieron.

17. It is still up in the air.	Eso no está decidido aún.
18.Time Is up.	Se acabó el tiempo
19.My computer is not working.	Mi computadora no funciona.
20. In a nutshell.	En conclusión.

Chapter 7

Chapter 7: Travel

Capítulo 7: Viajes

1.Where is…?	¿Dónde queda…?
2.What places can I visit?	¿Qué lugares puedo visitar?
3.Is it a safe place?	¿ Es un lugar seguro?
4. I would like to go to the beach.	Me gustaría ir a la playa.

5.Is there a good restaurant over there?	¿Qué restaurante bueno hay ahí?
6. I went to the airport to catch a flight to Colombia.	Fui al aeropuerto para tomar un vuelo a Colombia.
7.The airplane will land in two hours.	El avión va a aterrizar en dos horas.
8.Let me unpack my suitcase and then we can go swimming.	Dejame desempacar mi maleta y después vamos a nadar.
9.Where can I find…?	¿Dónde puedo encontrar…?
10.The trip to Bogotá was short.	El viaje a Bogotá estuvo corto. El viaje a Bogotá fue corto.
11. It's raining cats and dogs.	Está lloviendo a cantaros.
12. It's a nice day today.	Está haciendo un bonito día.
13. It's sunny.	Está haciendo sol.
14. Let's ride our bikes.	Montemos bicicleta.
15. I would like to ride the train.	Me gustaría tomar el tren.

16. Have you ever been a passenger on a ship?	¿Has montado en barco?
17. Do you know how to drive?	¿Sabes manejar?
18. I wouldn't advise you to go there.	No te aconsejaría ir allá.
19. I think traveling by bus is the best way.	Creo que ir en bus es lo mejor.
20. I hope you have fun.	Espero que te diviertas

Chapter 8

1. I know how to cook rice/meat/eggs/lentils/potatoes.	Sé preparar arroz/carne/huevos/lentejas/papas.
2.What dessert are you cooking?	¿Qué postre vas a preparar?
3.What did they order?	¿Qué pidieron en esa mesa?
4. I need corn/soy milk/beans/fish.	Necesito maíz/leche de soya/frijoles/pescado.

5. We are cooking chicken,tomatoes, onions, and lettuce salad.	Vamos a preparar pollo, ensalada con tomate, cebolla, y lechuga.
6. I would like to use sweet red pepper, and cauliflower.	Me gustaría usar pimentón, pepino y coliflor.
7.What ingredients do I need for fixing a guacamole?	¿Cuáles ingredientes necesito para preparar un guacamole?
8.You need avocado, cilantro,cebolla, lemon juice, salt, pepper, and tomato.	Necesitas aguacate, cilantro, cebolla, jugo de limón, sal, pimienta, y tomate.
9. What vegetarian/vegan foods do you know how to prepare?	¿Qué comidas vegetarianas/veganas sabes preparar?
10. I know how to cook tofu and hummus.	Sé preparar tofu.
11.What can we fix for breakfast?	¿Qué podemos hacer de desayuno?
12. I would like to have coffee, chocolate, fresh juice and eggs.	Me gustaría un café/chocolate/jugo de alguna fruta y huevos.
13.What fresh juice are you going to fix?	Vas a hacer jugo ¿De qué?

14. How do you want your eggs/steak cooked?	¿Cómo quieres los huevos/carne?
15. I want scrambled/sunny side up/omelets/soft-boiled/over-easy/ eggs.	Me gustan los huevos revueltos/fritos/ tibios.
16. The food is so good/yummy/tasty.	Te quedó deliciosa la comida.
17. Could you teach me how to cook…?	¿Me enseñas a preparar… ?
18. How do you want your steak cooked?	¿En que termino quiere la carne ?
19. I want my steak well done/medium well/medium rare/rare.	Quiero la carne bien/medio/un poquito roja/ roja/cocinada.
20. What sides do you want?	¿ Qué acompañantes quieres?

About the Author

Andrea Castellanos is a Spanish teacher in Denver, Colorado, U.S.

She is originally from Bogota, Colombia. She has 19+ years of teaching experience.

She holds a Bachelor's degree in Foreign Languages (English) and a Master's in Applied Linguistics. She is currently writing books for kids in Spanish.

Made in the USA
Middletown, DE
09 December 2023

45089099R00022